People of the Buffalo

People of the Buffalo

How the Plains Indians Lived

Maria Campbell

Illustrations by Douglas Tait & Shannon Twofeathers

FIREFLY BOOKS

A FIREFLY BOOK

To my grandson, Thomas John (T.J.), and the other children of his generation. Perhaps they will be completely liberated.

Copyright © Maria Campbell, 1976, 1983
Illustrations copyright © Douglas Tait and Shannon Twofeathers, 1976
First published in Canada by:
Douglas & McIntyre

This edition published in the United States in 1995 by:

Firefly Books (U.S.) Inc.
P.O. Box 1325
Ellicott Station
Buffalo, N.Y.
14205

Cataloguing in Publication Data

Campbell, Maria.
  People of the buffalo

ISBN 0-88894-329-6 (pbk.)

1. Indians of North America — Great Plains —
Juvenile literature. I. Tait Douglas.
II. Twofeathers, Shannon. III. Title.
IV. Series

E78.G73C34 1983   j978'.00497   C83-091281-9

Designed by Mike Yazzolino
Typeset by Domino-Link Graphic Communications Ltd.
Printed and bound in Canada by
D.W. Friesen & Sons Ltd.

Contents

Introduction

No other group in North America has been more misunderstood, romanticized and stereotyped than the Plains Indians, probably because of a lack of understanding and concern by the early travellers, missionaries and historians who tried to record the Indian culture and way of life without fully understanding it. They described the Plains Indians either as a childlike people who worshipped spirits or as bloodthirsty savages who liked bangles and beads. Books and films repeat the errors and misunderstandings.

Although this book tells how Indians lived, where they slept, what they ate, how they hunted—all the material things of their lives—you must bear in mind that they were deeply spiritual. It was not possible for Indians to separate their life as people do today into different categories such as work, play, religion, and art. To them, every part of life and all forms of life made up "the whole." To ignore one part was to lessen, even destroy one's self.

Area and Language

The plains is a geographical term used to describe the area between the Mississippi and the Rocky Mountains in the United States, and the southern part of Canada from the Rocky Mountains in Alberta to the Manitoba border. This land is short-grass country and prairie. There are few

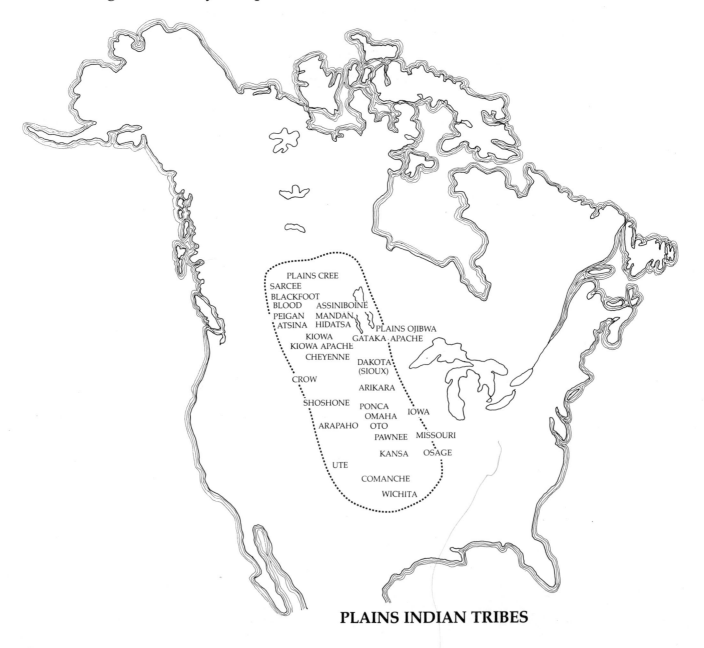

PLAINS INDIAN TRIBES

rivers or lakes. The climate is hot and dry in the summer and very cold in the winter. Because little rain falls, vegetation is stunted and few trees grow.

The plains people were as different in language and customs from other North American Indians as the Chinese are from the French. Plains tribes spoke dialects of six different root languages.

ROOT LANGUAGE	TRIBE	
Algonkian	Peigan	Plains Cree
	Blood	Plains Ojibwa
	Cheyenne	Blackfoot
	Arapaho	Atsina (or Gros Ventre)
Athapaskan	Sarcee	
	Kiowa Apache	
	Gataka Apache	
Caddoan	Arikara	
	Wichita	
	Pawnee	
Kiowan	Kiowa	
Shoshonean	Shoshone	
	Comanche	
	Ute	
Siouan	Crow	Dakota (or Sioux)
	Osage	Hidatsa
	Mandan	Assiniboine (or Stoney)
	Kansa	Missouri
	Iowa	Omaha
	Oto	Ponca

Although the plains tribes spoke different languages or dialects, they were of the same culture. They did not have a written language or even an alphabet, but they had various ways of communicating with each other. One of the common ways was sign language: speaking with the hands as mutes do. Smoke signals were used to announce news such as death or danger.

They mimicked birds and animals to alert each other in times of danger and also as a secret code. Drawings and symbols were used to record important events, especially visions, and were most often painted on buffalo robes or teepees.

Music often served as a sacred form of communication, for it was the language of the soul. The drum was especially important because it brought people together and it also represented the heartbeat of the universe.

BONE WHISTLE

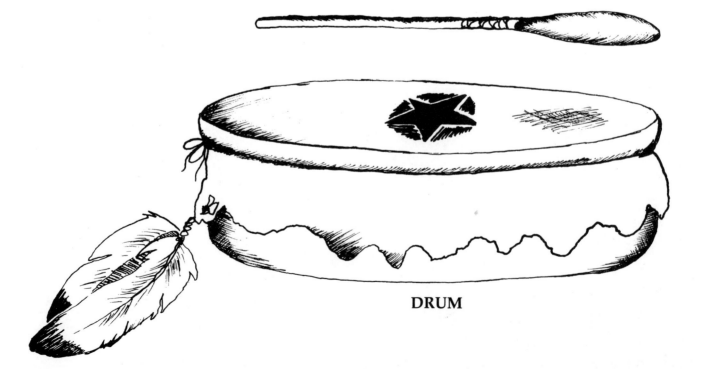

DRUM

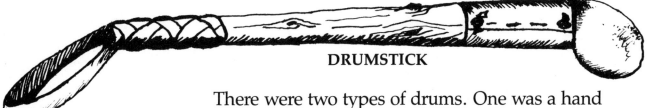

DRUMSTICK

There were two types of drums. One was a hand drum, made of rawhide stretched over a round wood frame and laced so that the drummer could hold it. The other, less common, was a hollowed-out section of tree not more than 60 cm high, with stretched rawhide on both ends laced tight with rawhide thongs.

Music was also made with rattles of rawhide stretched when wet over a small round or oblong wooden frame, with pebbles inside and a handle attached. Another instrument was the flute, made from hollowed-out willow sticks or bone. Whistles were made of the bone from a bird's wing.

On the lands occupied by the Plains Indians there were no artificial boundaries—no fences or walls—but each tribe kept to its own territory, and the edges of this territory were as clearly recognized as if a wall were actually there. An

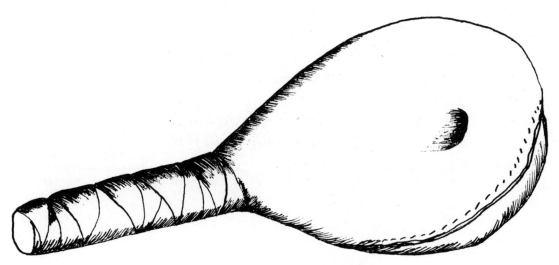

RATTLE

Indian would not cross a particular river, or an Indian hunter would hunt only part way up a hill, because to cross that water or go up that hill would put him into the territory of another tribe. It was believed that all souls have their own territory, and to invade another's knowingly and uninvited was wrong.

If an Indian hunted in another tribe's territory, he was punished by his own tribe, for he had endangered the safety of his own people. When it was necessary to make contact with another tribe—for example, to arrange a meeting—a small party was sent ahead to make preparations. Later, when horses became more common, raiding parties stole horses; this trespassing was something like a sport, but a dangerous one.

If a member of one tribe killed a member of another, the guilty person's family would have to punish the murderer, if necessary with death. Sometimes the family would surrender one of its members to be adopted as a replacement for the victim, if that was acceptable. Such an adoption was final, and the person adopted became a full member of his new family.

Similar adoptions took place between feuding families of the same tribe, and ensured that there would be no attempts at revenge.

Beliefs and ceremonies

The Plains Indians believed in a creator, sometimes called the Great Spirit. They also believed that all things had a soul, and so humans, animals, birds, fishes, plants and insects were treated with equal dignity and respect. The earth was recognized as the mother of all living things, and the sun, moon and stars were revered for their contribution to life.

The circle symbolized growth, for the Indian observed that all nature is a continuous round with no beginning or end. They saw this circle in their very existence with the cycle of birth, life and death. Man hunted animals to feed himself and his family, so animal nourished man; man grew old and returned to the earth to nourish the grass, which then fed the animal. Man therefore nourished the animal. The cycle was complete.

Because they recognized this natural dependency, there was no communication barrier. The plains people could call on other spirits in times of need: not so much by praying in the white man's sense but by fasting and meditating and being open to guiding signs from a helpful spirit.

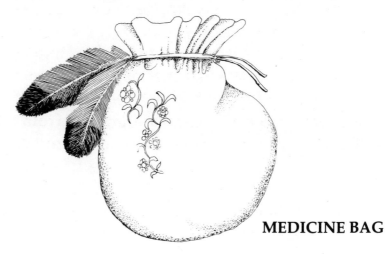

MEDICINE BAG

When young people reached puberty, they were considered adults and took their place as responsible members of the tribe.

A young man upon reaching puberty might go in search of a vision and a spirit protector of guardian. This quest was a very personal experience and was never taken lightly. A vision directed the course of his life and a spirit guardian protected him. Nothing was ever attempted without consulting the guardian and praying for wisdom and understanding.

To be a good warrior or chief meant to be spiritual and brave, and above all to live wisely with nature. There was no fear of death for the Indian, because he viewed death as only part of the cycle of life.

Meditation and solitude were important for everyone, as they kept the soul clean and strong. It was also good to laugh at one's self and to tell others in songs, dances and stories about one's mistakes and foolishness. Of course no one was good all the time, but those who were lazy, greedy or foolish did not survive for very long. If a person's behaviour harmed his people's way of life, he was forced to leave the camp and to fend for himself.

Tobacco smoking was a special ritual, not a habit. One early smoking mixture was made from red willow bark; later, tobacco was obtained from the Indians to the east. For the smoking ceremony, the participants sat in a circle. A pipe was filled and lit by the holder, who pointed it to the north and upwards to show respect for the Great Spirit (the creator), then to the four directions of the compass:

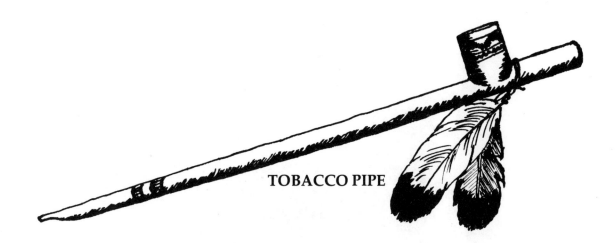

TOBACCO PIPE

east, south, west and north again. The pipe was passed clockwise around the circle. Tobacco was never smoked for pleasure, except by old people.

An infant's navel cord was cut immediately after birth and put into a small decorated bag that was retained for life, often worn around the neck. This was the individual's personal "medicine." Just as the navel cord provided the link between the baby in the womb and the woman who gave it life, so the medicine acted as a link between the person and the spiritual world. This medicine was not just a symbol, and its loss or destruction meant spiritual death.

When puberty was reached and a vision and a protector had been found, then the adult's medicine was strengthened by his selecting objects to make a medicine bundle. The objects might include a feather or a claw, if his protector was a bird, or there might be a flower if that had featured in his vision. The actual contents of the bundle were known only to the holder. As the owner matured and his spiritual strength became greater, the contents in the bundle were added to. The bundle was buried with its owner when he died, unless he had arranged to give it to a relative or friend, who would not know the contents but

CREE BUFFALO HEADDRESS

would simply add the bundle to his own, making his medicine stronger.

Medicine bundles were also held by Societies, but only the spiritual leaders of the Societies knew the contents. The Societies governed the tribe; there were Societies for warriors, for medicine people, for hunters and others. The Dog Soldiers, for example, were similar to policemen; they kept law and order in the community, during the hunt, on the march and at special ceremonies.

The Society was a sort of club where members could associate easily and exchange ideas about

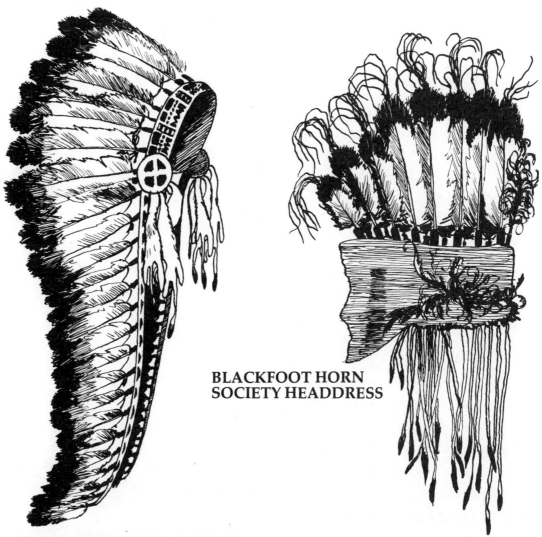

**BLACKFOOT HORN
SOCIETY HEADDRESS**

SIOUX CHIEF'S HEADDRESS

their special tasks. Membership in some Societies was hereditary, but if a young person born into one Society wanted to join another, he was free to do so. He would have to earn the membership and be sponsored by a member of the Society he wanted to join. For example, if he wanted to join the medicine Society he would approach a member who would be his teacher. When he had learned everything and showed that he would be a good medicine man, he could become a member. No one else could use his songs or dances unless he gave them, and this was a very special gift. In some tribes, songs and dances could be bought, but this only came about in very recent times.

No Plains Indian home was complete without sweetgrass, a fragrant grass that grows only in sacred places and cannot be found by everyone, even when it can be smelled in the air. The blades of sweetgrass are naturally tinted with purple and pink, and when braided and burned they give off smoke in a straight, fine, upward column. To make their sweetgrass incense, the Plains Indians braided freshly picked sweetgrass into a rope 12 mm to 25 mm in diameter and 25 cm to 60 cm long. The incense was used at all ceremonies and also by each individual who wanted to meditate in the home or sacred lodge. He would light a piece of the grass rope, hold his hands over the smoke and rub his body and hair with his hands. Then he would sit back and let the fragrance fill the air as he meditated. Dried sweetgrass was carried by everyone and there was some in every medicine bundle.

Throughout the year special ceremonies were held: some for thanksgiving, some to ask for guidance and good fortune, and others simply to share fun. All the ceremonies followed ritual strictly and were usually sponsored by a Society. Tribesmen especially looked forward to a celebration now called the pow-wow. It was held in the summer when tribes gathered from all over, shared their songs and dances, and visited old friends and relatives.

Many ceremonies were kept secret because they were sacred, and they remain so today.

The Family

Families were strong and closeknit, and old people were always treated with great respect. When they became very tired and ready to leave the world, they went away to die. No one tried to stop them, for the choice was theirs to make. But they remained important to the family as long as they lived.

Children were taught from birth by the old people to respect all living things, and probably because gentleness breeds gentleness, they were rarely punished or criticized severely. The old people also taught them how to use tools and how to hunt, so that by the time they reached puberty they had learned to be adults.

Brothers and sisters were taught to protect each other. Aunts and uncles were like second parents and were important, because a child could confide in them as adult friends. If a parent died, an aunt or uncle took over the responsibility of the dead parent. Cousins were as brothers and sisters, and all great aunts and great uncles were regarded as grandparents.

Marriages between blood relatives, even distant ones, were taboo. However, marriages between relatives by marriage were not frowned upon; in fact, such marriages were common, for if a man married his brother's widow the children gained a familiar father and the widow was not left to fend for herself. A man might marry his wife's sister and have two wives, but it was his wife who first made the proposal and then only if the husband agreed.

In a first marriage, the bride was usually chosen by the man, whose family then offered gifts and

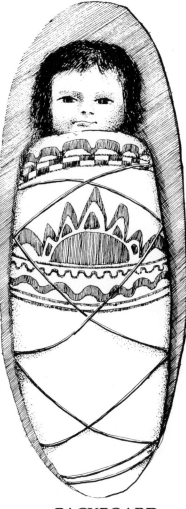

PACKBOARD

made arrangements with the girl's parents. If the girl's family did not approve, or if the girl was opposed to the match, the gifts were returned. It was not often that a girl refused to marry her parents' choice, but her refusal was respected.

If after marriage the couple had problems that they could not overcome, they separated. Although separation was not encouraged, it was not considered as bad as continuing an unsuccessful marriage.

Great respect was shown to in-laws, especially to mothers and fathers. After marriage a man had to show how important and powerful his wife's

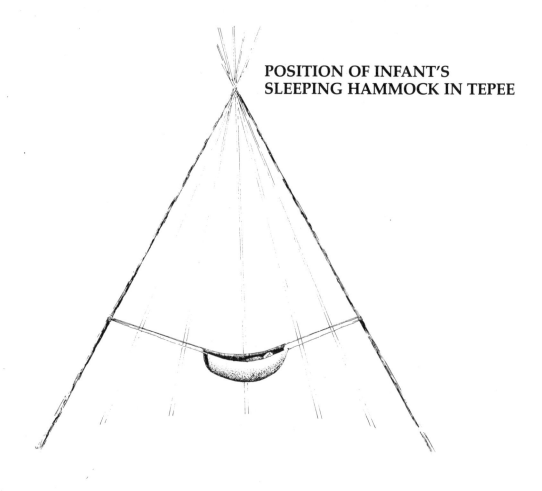

POSITION OF INFANT'S SLEEPING HAMMOCK IN TEPEE

mother was: he could not speak directly to her, look at her, or use her name. The same rigid rules applied to his wife in regard to her father-in-law. The rules were not as rigid towards other members of the family. Usually the man lived with his wife's people, but in the Blackfoot tribes the woman went to live with her in-laws.

A newborn baby was cleaned and put into a bag full of soft moss that acted as a diaper and provided warmth. The bag was slung from the mother's back; when she was busy she hung it from a peg in the tepee or from a special post outside. During the night the child slept in a hammock that was slung over the mother's bed and was rocked when the infant cried.

Soon after birth a feast was held, and the baby given a name by a relative, who would from then on be a second mother or father. A boy's adult name was decided after he had had his vision at puberty; a medicine man interpreted the vision and then named the boy.

To see a vision and a spirit guardian, the boy went away from the camp and the people, cleansed his body in a sweat lodge and fasted and meditated. He did this until he found what he was seeking. If unsuccessful, and too weak to continue, he would go home and try again later. This was not considered a failure but only meant that he was not yet ready.

Plains Indian girls did not have to seek a vision at puberty. The menstrual cycle brought power to communicate freely with the spirits, whereas a boy had to seek them.

The young girl was lodged in a tepee away from the camp, where she was guarded for four days by an old medicine woman who could communicate with and control the spirits. The girl could not go near sacred objects such as medicine pipes or bundles during this time, because of the uncontrolled spirits around her.

During these four days the girl was taught the ritual she must follow each month, and the meaning and purpose of it. Her training under the old medicine woman also taught her how to control the spirits so that they could not take over her mind.

When the four days were over, she was brought back to camp and a feast was held in her honour, at which time gifts were given to all the guests. In some tribes, she was then given an adult name. This name was given to her by the old woman who taught her, and usually the name was of significance; "Red Stone Woman" could mean that her power and guardian was a red stone.

A woman was seen to be like nature with its seasons, the strongest time in her life being during puberty and after middle age. The time in between was for the giving of new life. Some people think that in the Indian way of life the boy was glorified; on the contrary, the girl was considered spiritually stronger, because like the earth she gives life. Boys and girls were treated equally, and were not criticized if they chose work that was unusual for their sex: some women hunted and rode in battle, and some men cooked and tanned hides.

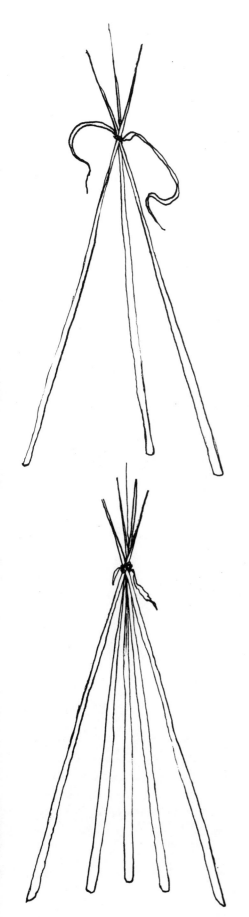

Shelter

The Plains Indians lived in tepees, cone-shaped tents covered with buffalo hides. A tepee was started by lashing three or four poles together with rawhide thongs; then the poles were raised to make a stand. The thongs that tied the poles together were long enough to reach the ground, where they were staked outside the tepee to provide support.

Thirteen poles or more, depending on the size wanted, were leaned counterclockwise around the stand, and covered with twelve to twenty buffalo skins which had been sewn together with sinew. This cover was drawn tightly around the poles and then pinned together with wooden pegs.

BUFFALO-SKIN TEPEE

PLACING POLES FOR TEPEE

TEPEES AND DRYING RACK

The fireplace was in the centre of the tepee, with
a hole at the top for a chimney. Atop two opposite
poles leaning against the tepee, flaps were attached.
Moved on these poles, the flaps covered or
uncovered the hole to control the heat and smoke or
keep out snow.

The door faced east to greet the sun and the birth
of a new day. Across from the door was the place of
honour. Scattered around the floor were woven
willow back rests, which were like chairs without
legs. The sleeping area was covered with buffalo
robes. Against the walls were containers and bags
used for storing food, clothing and the personal
belongings of the family.

The outside of the tepee was painted by the man of the family, either with designs given to him in a dream or vision or with pictures telling of his skills as a warrior or hunter. Near the tepee stood a pole or tripod from which hung the medicine that protected him, his home and family.

The tepees were set in a circle, the circle being a symbol of the cycle of life, and were always situated near wooded areas close to water. Tepee poles, which were awkward to carry, might be left behind when the people moved in search of game and berries, for they always returned to the same campsites.

PLAINS INDIAN CAMPSITE

Food

The buffalo provided the plains people with their main source of food. When a herd was sighted, the medicine man of the tribe would call all the people together to dance to the Buffalo Spirit for a successful hunt. After the ceremony the hunting party would set out.

There were two main ways to take the buffalo. Before the introduction of the horse, the hunters would creep up on the herd from all sides, then rush in, simultaneously firing their arrows. With the coming of the horse, they ran the animals down on horseback and shot their arrows on the gallop.

The second way was the jumping pound. This method was the most effective, since they could run a whole winter's supply of meat over an embankment, most often a riverbank.

BUFFALO

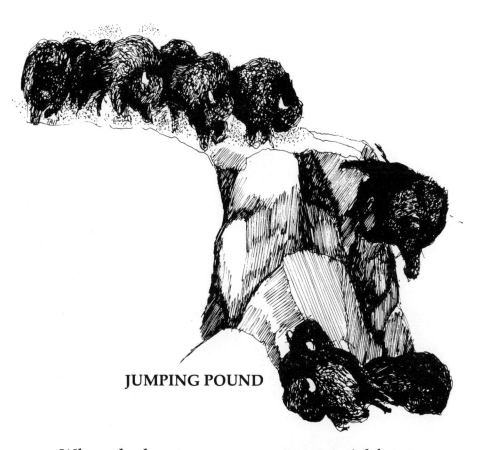

JUMPING POUND

When the hunt was over, a ceremonial feast was held, with the choicest meats given to the aged, widows and orphans. Tobacco would be offered to the Buffalo Spirit for giving itself to the people. The scent bag, the buffalo's scrotum, would be returned to the earth as a gesture of respect and thanksgiving.

RABBIT SNARE

COOKING

Preparing the meat and hides for the entire camp was done by women, children, and the men who chose to stay home from the hunt. This work could take weeks to complete. The meat would be cut up and hung on huge willow racks to smoke and dry. When it was ready, it was stored in bags or containers made from the skins of buffalo or other game.

Some of the dried meat was put on a flat hollowed-out rock and pounded with a round rock until it was shredded, after which it was mixed with animal fat. For a special treat, berries might be added. This nutritious mixture was called pemmican. It would keep for long periods of time and was easy to carry on hunting trips.

The Indians supplemented their buffalo meat diet with other game and fowl such as antelope, deer, rabbits, prairie chickens, partridge, ducks and geese. Occasionally fish were caught with a small net woven from the inner bark of the red willow.

SMOKING FISH

Berries, wild turnips, roots and herbs were also picked, usually by the women and children. The berries were dried and stored in skin containers. The wild turnips were peeled and dried, then pounded to a fine flour and used as thickening for soups.

Meat was usually roasted over an open fire, but boiling water for soups and stews was obtained by setting hot rocks on top of a willow rack inside a skin cooking pot filled with water. Wild turnip powder would thicken the broth, and herbs or roots seasoned the food to make it tasty.

Storage and Utensils

The buffalo provided the plains people with food, shelter and clothing. It also provided them with material to make many of their utensils and tools.

Food and clothing were stored in boxes, containers and bags made from the hides of the buffalo and other small game. Sometimes the skin was cured with the fur or hair left on, but usually the fur was scraped off to make rawhide.

Rawhide was cut and sewn into the shape and size of container needed, and left to dry. The stomachs of small game made excellent airtight bags having many uses.

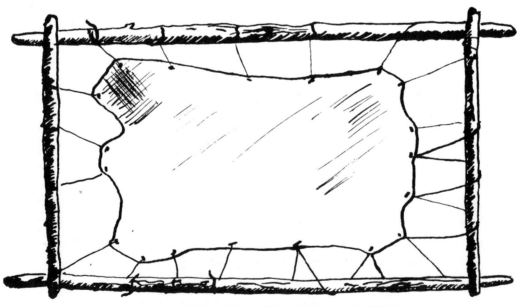

TANNING FRAME FOR BUFFALO HIDE

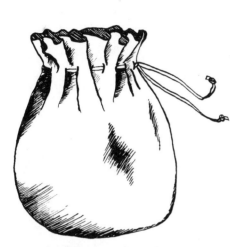

STORAGE POUCH

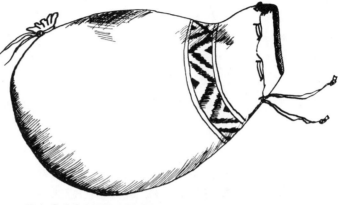

BAG MADE FROM ANIMAL STOMACH

Cooking pots were similar to those used for storing, but were fashioned around a willow frame to prevent the pot from collapsing when it was wet.

Containers and baskets were made from birch bark and sewn with spruce roots, but they were rare among the plains people. Occasionally they wove willow baskets, but these were cumbersome and so were not very popular.

FRAME FOR COOKING POT

SKIN COOKING POT

NEEDLE

Sinew, used for sewing and for many other purposes, is the back muscle of an animal. It is long and stringy; when separated and dried it makes an excellent thread, and is almost impossible to break. Many craftsmen today still use sinew because of its strength.

Glue was obtained by boiling hooves or horns to a fine paste.

Scrapers and fleshers for scraping flesh and fat off hides were made from the thigh and leg bones of animals. Their edges were serrated.

Needles and awls were carved from slivers of bone or horn. The sliver was smoothed and shaped to a fine point and a hole drilled at the end for the thread. Awls were used for punching holes in hide.

Bones from rabbits and other small game were hollowed out and cleaned and, when plugged at each end, were ideal for storing needles.

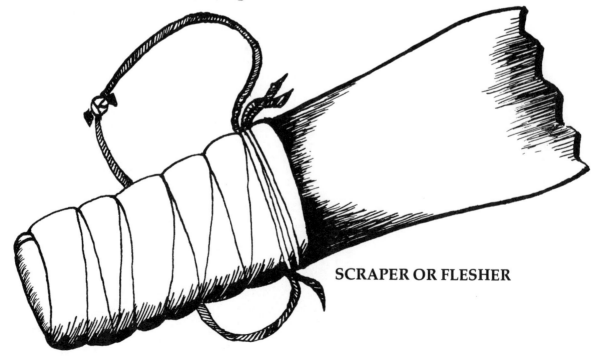

SCRAPER OR FLESHER

BUFFALO HORN SPOON

Eating bowls were made from hollowed-out wood, and sometimes from bark. Because wood and bark were rare on the plains, these dishes were highly prized.

Knives were carved from the ribs of animals, and sometimes the blade was made from chipped flint tied to a bone handle.

Rocks and stone utensils were also used, including round and oblong stone mauls and flat hollowed-out rocks for the preparation of pemmican, wild turnips or crushed berries. The stone maul usually fitted inside the hollow.

The women decorated the containers and utensils with colourful designs.

BONE KNIFE

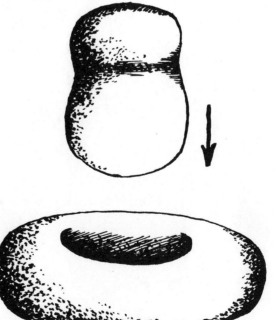

STONE MAUL AND HOLLOWED-OUT ROCK

Clothing

The Plains Indians wore clothing made from
dressed hides. Preparing the hides for the clothing
was a long, backbreaking process. The fresh wet
hide was stretched and pegged to the ground or
stretched on a rack. It was scraped clean of fat and
flesh and then soaked in a pool of water for three
days or until the hair or fur began to slip off. It was
stretched again and the remaining hair scraped off.
After drying, the hide was rubbed with a prepared
mixture of sand and animal brains, and again left to
dry. In the final stage the hide was worked by
rubbing it together until it was soft and pliable.
Sometimes the finished product was tanned light
brown or it was coloured with natural dyes.

MAN'S SHIRT

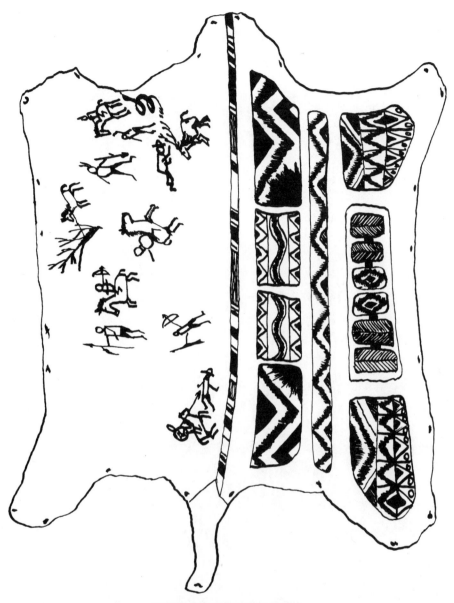

DECORATED ROBE

Dyes were obtained from plants or minerals, such as iron ore for a reddish colour. From other minerals came green, blue, yellow, orange and purple. Powdered coal, charcoal and soot black were also used, as well as crushed berries and rushes. Because the Indians lived so close to nature, they observed how she blended her colours and blended theirs in the same way.

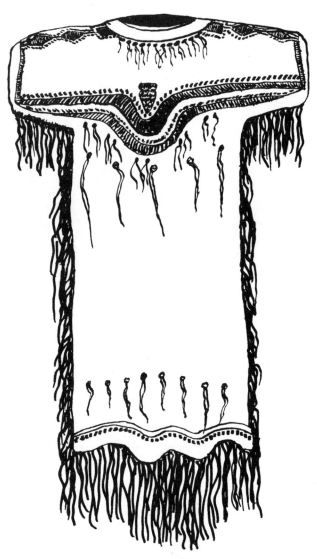

ELK-HIDE DRESS

All the sewing was done with sinew, using an awl or a bone needle. The decorating of clothing was done with dyed porcupine quills and later, with dyed horse hair and beads. There is probably no finer example of quill work or the blending of natural dyes anywhere in the world.

The tails of animals such as weasels and foxes were used for decorations, as were shells, claws, feathers and hooves. Jewellery was also made from these materials.

FUR WRAPAROUND HAT

BUCKSKIN LEGGING

The plains people used body paint on special occasions such as death or sickness, and the painted designs had special significance.

The elaborate costuming that is seen today was developed only in the last hundred years with the availability of the white man's clothing and such materials as beads and dyed feathers. The ceremonial costumes worn by chicken dancers or eagle dancers were not as flamboyant as those seen today and were reserved for religious gatherings and dances, not for just any gathering.

The women wore long fringed and decorated dresses which extended from the chin to the feet. They wore knee high leggings and moccasins. In the winter months a fur robe was also worn.

MOCCASIN VAMP DESIGN

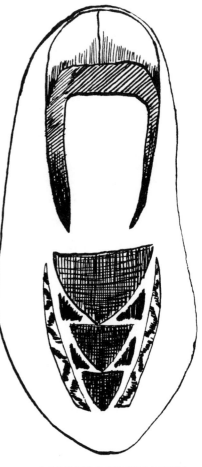

MAN'S MOCCASIN

The men wore a fringed shirt, a breechcloth or a pair of aprons, and moccasins. In the winter they wore a fur robe, leggings that reached the hips, and fur-lined moccasins much higher than those worn for summer.

Blankets or robes were traditional overgarments long before the coming of the white traders. The robe, which was sometime furred, was made pliable and soft by dressing and tanning the pelts of foxes, wolves and other animals, and sewing together the finished pelts. The buffalo robe was also prepared in this way. Sometimes fur and bird feathers were woven together to make a robe.

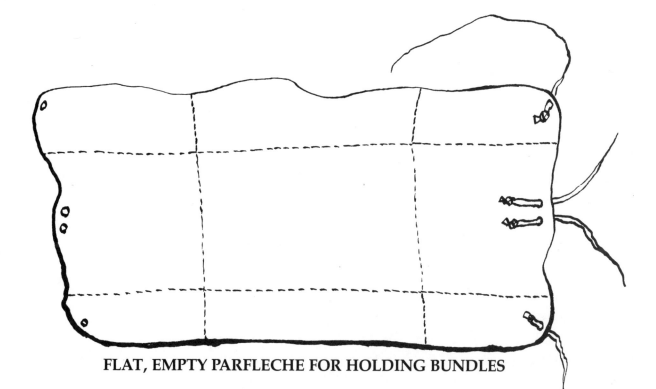

FLAT, EMPTY PARFLECHE FOR HOLDING BUNDLES

PARFLECHE, FOLDED AND TIED

The Indians wore fur hats in the winter and went bareheaded in the summer. The elaborate headdresses such as war bonnets and buffalo heads were worn only by a select few and only on special occasions. Only chiefs, medicine men and those belonging to societies wore the headdresses. Warriors wore feathers, but these had to be earned by an honourable deed.

Transportation

The plains tribes were nomadic and travelled almost constantly, following the great buffalo herds within their territories.

In early times dogs were used to transport their possessions. The dogs, which were about the size of a wolf, were trained to pull a travois, which consisted of two poles tied together at the top with rawhide, and attached to the dog's shoulders. The ends dragged on the ground behind the dog. Halfway down and between these two poles a rawhide net was woven, and to this frame loads of up to 30 kg were tied. In this way meat, firewood, small children and family possessions were transported. Many families had as many as twenty dogs. Later when the horse was introduced, a larger travois was used for the same purpose.

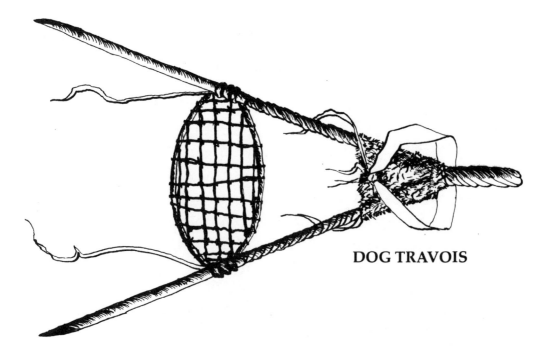

DOG TRAVOIS

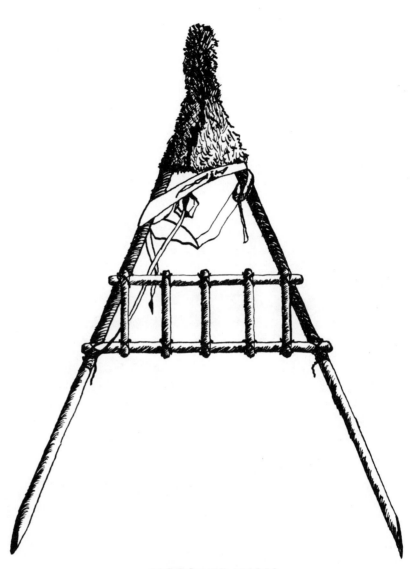

HORSE TRAVOIS

Horses were introduced to the Plains Indians sometime in the early seventeenth century; nearly all the plains people had horses. It was at this time that the life of the Plains Indians began to change.

Having horses meant that hunting was done much faster and more efficiently. Travel also became faster, and distances covered increased, so that trading with other tribes became more frequent. Up to this time, wealth and prestige had not been of importance, but the number of horses owned and the acquisition of trade goods became a measure of wealth and prestige.

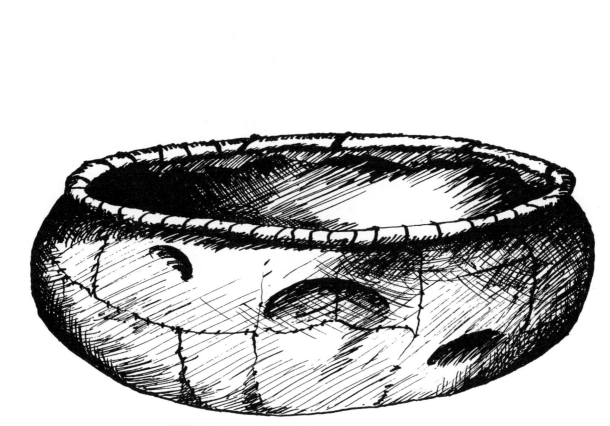

BULL BOAT OF SKIN OVER WILLOW FRAME

Bark and dugout canoes were seldom used by the plains people; skin-covered boats or rafts were constructed to ferry possessions across a stream or river. Rafts were often towed by strong swimmers.

Snowshoes were used by some of the tribes, especially those close to the foothills. The frames were made of birch and were shaped by boiling the wood until it was flexible and could be shaped. Then they were woven with wet rawhide like snowshoes today.

Warfare

The weapons of the Plains Indians were few but effective, the bow and arrow being the primary weapon. The bow was considered a sacred weapon because its shape is part of a circle. It was made from gray willow or saskatoon, which were abundant on the plains and used for many things. A sapling or branch, usually about a metre long, was split and put three times through a process of boiling, shaping and drying. This tempered the wood, making it stronger and much easier to work with. The grip was wrapped with rawhide to prevent the hand from slipping when the bow was pulled; the string was made of sinew.

CROW SHIELDS, PAINTED

The arrows were made of thin willow saplings or branches, and as these were rarely straight, they went through the same process of boiling and shaping. To make their arrowheads, hunters selected flint or other hard rock. They shaped and sharpened an arrowhead by chipping with a sharp hard rock or by heating it, then dripping cold water onto it to make the edges flake. Feathers were attached to the butt end of the arrows to help them fly true; their range was up to 15 m.

Blunt arrows were used to hunt small game and fowl, and sharp arrows to hunt big game. Bow cases and quivers were made from rawhide and cured animal skins.

Clubs were used only occasionally. They were made by encasing a round stone in a rawhide bag which was attached to a wooden handle so as to be very flexible. The club's handle had a rawhide loop at the other end, so that it could be carried wrapped around the wrist.

RAWHIDE-WRAPPED WAR CLUB

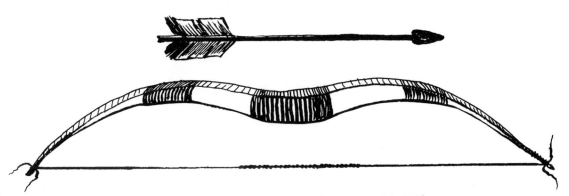

SINEW-BACKED BOW (BLACKFOOT)

Spears and lances had shafts of gray willow or saskatoon tree, and tips of sharp bone or flint.

A warrior fashioned his shield from the tough neckhide of a bull. It could ward off arrows but was also a symbolic protector. The protection it provided was in the powers that its owner believed lay in the designs and colours used to decorate the shield; these came to him in a dream or vision. On the shield he hung feathers or furs from his spirit guardian for further protection.

A man could never kill the bird or animal that was his guardian or protector, apart from the pelt or bird attached to his shield, and then only because the creature willingly gave itself to him.

Before the coming of the white man, violence was not common, and tribes did not declare war on each other. If laws were broken, the guilty parties were punished, with death if necessary, for jeopardizing the safety of the tribe.

If there was fighting, then rather than killing each other, warriors might "count coup," which was the repeated touching of the enemy with a coup stick,

PLAINS INDIAN SPEAR

MOUNTED WARRIOR WITH SPEAR

each strike being counted. All tribes on the plains honoured this chivalry, but when the white man came, he did not understand or honour the coup stick; he killed with his gun.

The Indian respected the sacredness of death and left the body of an enemy to its family. Hair was never touched, as it especially was considered sacred. Scalping was encouraged by the white man: the French paid the Indians with whiskey and trade goods for British scalps, and the British did the same for French scalps.

Epilogue

The Plains Indian met the white man as a brother. He fed and clothed him, as this was part of his religion. When the white man gave him gifts, he accepted them, for this too was traditional. He gave furs in exchange for beads, axes and cloth. Soon he was indebted to the white man, who then wanted more furs. It was no longer a friendly exchange, but a business.

To get more fur, the people had to extend their hunting territory; this caused bad feelings among the tribes, and eventually wars. Whiskey was introduced and the resulting drunkenness weakened the Indian's spiritual strength. Guns encouraged violence and killing. Christianity caused confusion of beliefs in an already spiritually weakened society. The result was poverty of life and of the spirit.

The Indian was forced to live by the white man's law which gave his land to the increasing number of white settlers. By the time the Indian understood what was happening to him, it was too late.

Today Indian people are fighting back by using the laws that almost destroyed them, but most important of all they are going back to their spiritual way of life. That is the most important weapon of all: to know who you are and where you come from.